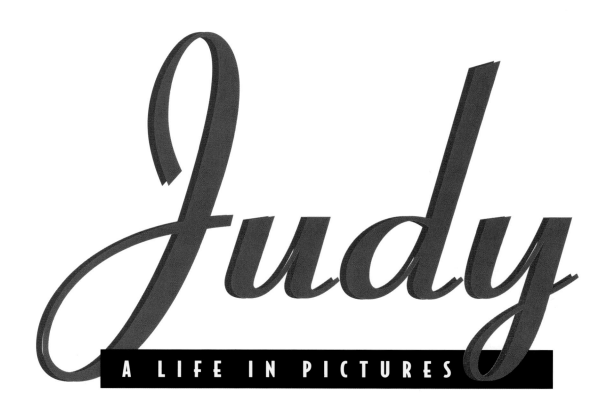

Judy

A LIFE IN PICTURES

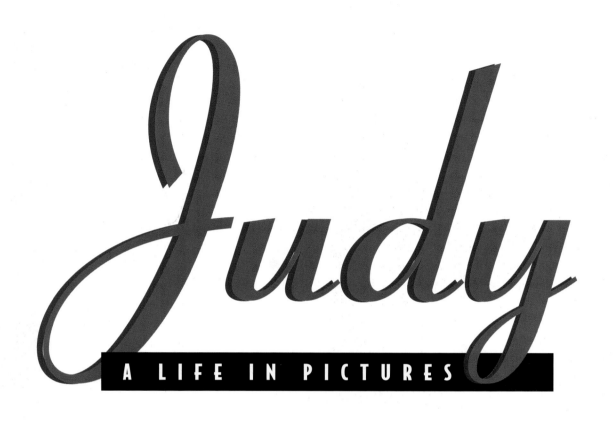

Judy

A LIFE IN PICTURES

BASIL NESTOR

MetroBooks

MetroBooks

An Imprint of Friedman/Fairfax Publishers

© 1997 by Michael Friedman Publishing Group, Inc.

Library of Congress Cataloging-in-Publication Data available upon request.

ISBN 1-56799-436-9

Editor: Stephen Slaybaugh
Art Director: Kevin Ullrich
Designer: Millie Sensat
Photography Editor: Deidra Gorgos

Color separations by Ocean Graphics International Company Ltd.
Printed in China by Leefung-Asco Printers

10 9 8 7 6 5 4 3 2 1
For bulk purchases and special sales, please contact:
Friedman/Fairfax Publishers
Attention: Sales Department
15 West 26th Street
New York, NY 10010
212/685-6610 FAX 212/685-1307

Visit our website: http://www.metrobooks.com

Dedication

This book is dedicated to my mom who, like Judy Garland, is not perfect, but is beautiful, inspiring, and loves her children.

Acknowledgments

Thanks to: Marilyn Thibodaux and Jeff Kent for their advice and patience; Carrie Allen for her faith and perseverance; Hope Murray for her boundless spirit and insight; Sylvia Jackson Miller for sharing with me her precious Judy Garland memorabilia; Tom Hansen for always being there; Stephen Slaybaugh for being an outstanding book editor; and Deidra Gorgos for being a resourceful photo editor. Extra special thanks to Merv Griffin who taught me to understand talent by sharing with me his own genius.

CONTENTS

Introduction

Above: This is the way most of the world remembers Judy Garland: singing "Over The Rainbow," either on film or in concert. It is amazing to think MGM executives almost cut the song from *The Wizard of Oz*. The fact that they didn't speaks much about the inexplicable force that drove Judy Garland's life. Judy's fortune was always brilliance pulled from uncertainty. Her life was a series of inspired moments born of confusion and discord (in later years the discord was often instigated by Judy herself). She loved the extreme and instinctively understood that the emotion of wanting to be over the rainbow is infinitely more stirring than being there.

Opposite: The result of Judy's come-from-behind karma was a bewitching public persona. She wasn't a beauty in the classic sense, but she radiated a vulnerability that made her irresistible. People (especially the men she would marry) were unceasingly inspired to wrap Judy in their arms and take care of her. That is certainly what Judy wanted, yet she chafed at the restrictions those relationships produced. Whether it was MGM, television, or marriage, her alliances were always tempestuous.

She is by any measure an astonishing character in the history of entertainment. Judy Garland lived only forty-seven years, but compressed in that short time were many lifetimes' worth of accomplishments. She was most obviously an incomparable singer, her voice so outstanding that Hedda Hopper described it as "clear as a golden trumpet." Judy was a Hollywood star of the highest stature: her filmography is a litany of milestones including *Meet Me in St. Louis*, *Harvey Girls*, *For Me and My Gal*, *Easter Parade*, *Summer Stock*, *A Star Is Born*, and the perennial *The Wizard of Oz*.

Judy danced with Fred Astaire, Gene Kelly, Ray Bolger, and Cyd Charisse. She had an amazing comic ability and timing that made her the perfect screen foil (and screen equal) for comedy legend Mickey Rooney. She was a dramatic actress, twice nominated for an Oscar as an adult and recipient of a special Oscar in 1939 for her performance in *The Wizard of Oz*.

Judy Garland had a full career in motion pictures as a child star, effortlessly made the often difficult transition to adult star, then extended her professional successes (and cemented her position in the international psyche) by returning to her vaudeville roots, the live stage. And if that weren't enough, she worked on radio, had her own television series, and recorded dozens of albums and hit singles, including "Over the Rainbow," and "For Me and My Gal." For most performers succeeding in just one of these areas of accomplishment would fill a lifetime. Judy did them all.

The sheer scope of her work is stunning, especially in light of the difficulties she faced throughout her life. The most publicized, of course, were her habitual troubles with alcohol and drugs. Chemical abuse contributed to her departure from MGM, the demise of her career, and eventually her death. But pills and alcohol were only the catalyst for her problems. The source of the trouble lay near the source of the greatness. Judy loved to perform.

She performed brilliantly for the screen and just as brilliantly (and often destructively) in her personal life, too. She suffered a panoply of legitimate physical ailments. Headaches, earaches, stomachaches, sore throats, sleepless nights, fatigue, and countless other illnesses plagued her. Doctors would confirm she was ill and unable to work, yet she worked. When she didn't, she might appear hours later at a popular nightspot or private party and sing until dawn. Which was the real Judy Garland? Was she sick? Healthy? Happy? Unhappy? Helpless? Running the show?

The paradoxical answer is, all of the above. She wasn't acting— or perhaps she was. It was all true, including the contradictions. She was the girl next door who just happened to dance beautifully

opposite Fred Astaire. She was the regular girl from the Midwest who broke our hearts singing "Over the Rainbow." Enchantment like that requires—in fact, demands—a fuzzing of reality.

As her daughter Liza Minnelli once aptly put it: "Anybody who really knew her knew what a funny, bright, witty raconteur she was. Her vocabulary was immense, and she had a way of telling a story. She could change anything. So anything she talked about would become an epic."

Judy Garland was herself epic. Her ability to effortlessly lift the mundane to the momentous made her one of the most incandescent performers of the twentieth century. She burned bright and hot, and although she eventually burned out, her tremendous cre-

Left: This early promotional photo demonstrates MGM's initial confusion regarding how to publicly present Judy. Should she be an adorable child or a beguiling teen? Neither seemed appropriate. Judy herself suffered greatly over this situation. Of her first MGM film performance she said, "When I saw a chubby, freckle-faced, snub-nosed little girl on the screen, and I realized I was looking at myself, I went home and cried myself to sleep." This harsh sentiment and MGM's uncertainty belies the affection and respect Judy engendered for herself during her first year at the studio. Though she was virtually ignored by Louis B. Mayer, her collection of influential fans included screenwriter (and later director) Joseph Mankiewicz, Ida Koverman (assistant to Louis B. Mayer), and composer/arranger/producer Roger Edens who was instrumental in Judy's musical career.

ative light still shines, nearly fifty years after her last picture for MGM and almost three decades after her death. To this day, no performer in the world can sing "Over The Rainbow," "Get Happy," "The Man That Got Away" or a dozen other songs without conjuring the spirit of Judy Garland.

Judy is still very much with us and in us. She is us as a child when she speaks the words imprinted on our hearts: "There's no place like home." She is us as a fresh-faced teen with energy and a dream to "put on a show." She is us as a young adult looking forward to a storybook future where "all our troubles will be out of sight." And she is definitely us as an adult, dressed as a tramp still reaching for the rainbow.

The story of Judy Garland is not the story of chemical abuse or too many husbands. It is not a list of box office achievements, a roster of hit films, a schedule of concert dates, or an index of pop-culture high points. The real story of Judy Garland is the tale of an exceptional woman who genuinely touched the lives of millions of people. It is the story of a person who laughed, cried, screamed, loved, and died in the public eye. This book is a chronicle of that story—it is an unabashed celebration of the wonder of Judy Garland.

Chapter One

Baby Gumm

Above: She was born Frances Ethel Gumm on June 10, 1922, but her family called her "Baby." Baby's parents, Frank and Ethel, were theater folk in Grand Rapids, Minnesota. Frank was "singer and manager" at the New Grand Theater. Ethel played piano. Baby had two older sisters, Mary Jane and Dorothy Virginia.

The youngest Gumm made her stage debut at the New Grand on December 26, 1924. Baby sang with her sisters, danced, and then did a solo of "Jingle Bells." She held a handbell and rang it enthusiastically after each line. The audience went wild. Baby basked in the applause and did an encore—and then another, and still another. Each time was louder and more spirited than the one before. Finally her grandmother (some accounts say her father) strode onto the stage and bundled Baby off. She was still singing and ringing the bell as she disappeared behind the curtain.

Opposite: The grown up Judy Garland always remembered the lessons of that first stage experience. Years later she reflected, "To this day whenever an enthusiastic audience gives me that 'wanting to sing all night' feeling, I hear the first notes of 'Jingle Bells' and make a quick exit."

Ambition and warm weather brought the Gumms to California in 1926. Frank leased a theater just north of Los Angeles in Lancaster. Ethel shuttled Frances and her sisters to Los Angeles for auditions and performances and to attend Ethel Meglin's Dance Studio, a well-known school for child performers.

Frances made her screen debut in *The Big Review* (shown here), a 1929 talkie short that featured "Ethel Meglin's Famous Hollywood Wonder Kids." Baby Gumm danced and sang with her sisters and easily stole the spotlight. Even in this early period, reviewers of her performances saw (and heard) what would eventually be Judy Garland's trademarks. One reporter wrote that little Frances "shook these well-known rafters with her songs...." *Variety* called her the "selling end of a trio."

Above: Ethel (here with Judy in a 1940 photo) vigorously promoted "The Gumm Sisters." Frank objected when the bookings and other activities separated the family. The parents argued, their disagreements exacerbated by financial pressures brought on by the deepening Depression. Frank's theater began to lose money. The arguments worsened and partially led to Judy's later statement that her mother was "the real Wicked Witch of the West."

Left: Yet it was undoubtedly Ethel Gumm who took the pivotal steps that would shape Judy Garland (pictured). In 1934 Ethel booked The Gumm Sisters (again over Frank's objections) on a tour that took them from Denver to Chicago. They performed in the Windy City with George Jessel. He didn't like the name Gumm, so he fancifully introduced them as "The Garland Sisters." The family embraced the moniker. Gumm was gone.

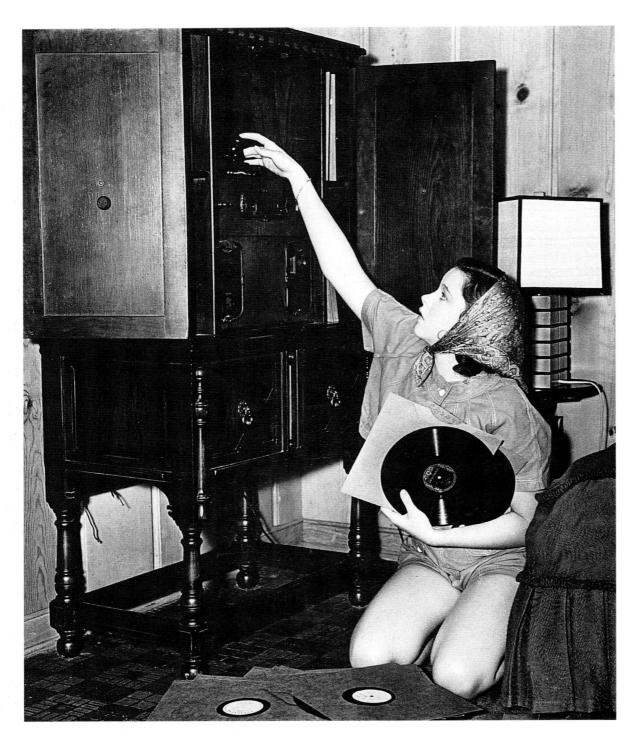

Left: In the next few months the girls changed their first names. Mary Jane became Suzy. Virginia became Jimmy. Frances chose Judy because she liked the line in a Hoagy Carmichael song that went, "If you think she's a saint and find out she ain't, that's Judy."

Destiny began to work its magic when Marc Rabwin, a family friend, introduced the Garlands to Joe Mankiewicz. At the time Mankiewicz was working as a writer for MGM. When he heard Judy sing, he was stunned, and later recalled that her voice was "something incredible even then." He wanted to see Judy signed at MGM.

Opposite: Judy was, as Hedda Hopper described, "a roly poly girl with eyes like saucers." In the heyday of Shirley Temple, Judy was not the sort of child to make Hollywood jump. Still Mankiewicz persisted. Getting Judy signed at MGM meant getting approval from Louis B. Mayer, the studio head. Mankiewicz invited Ida Koverman, Mayer's assistant, to hear Judy sing. Koverman was impressed.

What happened next has been described in so many ways it is now difficult to distinguish the truth. Various people have claimed credit for getting Judy signed with MGM. We know she auditioned more than once, but who at the studio approved her contract? Did Louis B. Mayer ever attend an audition? What is certain is that on September 27, 1935 Judy Garland began her career as an employee of MGM.

A sad postscript; two months later Frank died suddenly of spinal meningitis. He was forty-nine.

Chapter Two

Dorothy and Andy Hardy

Opposite: *Every Sunday* (1936), a one-reel short, was Judy's first effort for MGM (nearly a year after she was signed). It was designed to showcase Judy and another young contract singer, Deanna Durbin (standing). Mayer liked the result, but was angered to learn Durbin's contract with MGM had expired. Universal snapped her up and Durbin soon starred in the hit film *Three Smart Girls* (1936).

Above: Judy was loaned to Twentieth Century Fox for *Pigskin Parade* (1936). She was nearly last on the list of featured players, below Arline Judge and Dixie Dunbar. The reviews were favorable and the picture made money, but that was little consolation to the girl who had stardom as a goal. Judy had no idea she was on her way to the highest echelon of celebrity, far beyond the achievements of contemporaries like Deanna Durbin.

Left: Clark Gable's thirty-sixth birthday party is where the rocket ride to the top began. It was an elaborate affair held on the set of *Parnell* (1937). The entertainment included Judy singing "Dear Mr. Gable" (popularly known as "You Made Me Love You"). Gable was so moved that he cried. Word of the astounding performance spread. When Judy repeated the performance at MGM's annual meeting of exhibitors, the audience went wild.

Right: Judy and "Dear Mr. Gable" were quickly incorporated into MGM's *Broadway Melody of 1938* (1937). The result is one of cinema's most stirring moments. Judy plays an adoring fan singing to a photo of Clark Gable. The quality of her voice and the brilliance of her phrasing pierced the heart and brought many theater patrons, like Gable, to tears.

Above: Judy performed an enchanting dance with Buddy Ebsen (shown here) and conducted a hilarious sing-along with Sophie Tucker, aptly titled "Everybody Sing," in *Broadway Melody of 1938*. The rest of the film (starring Robert Taylor and Eleanor Powell) is an interesting contrast to Judy's performance. It's as if an emotional switch goes on the moment Judy appears. She stole the film to such an extent that *Variety* called the non-Garland portions "filler."

For nearly two years there had been little for Judy to do at MGM. Suddenly she was recognized as a potential star, and there was everything to do. She was quickly rushed into two pictures shot simultaneously. *Thoroughbreds Don't Cry* (1937) was so hastily written and produced Judy had only one song. The film is mostly memorable because it paired Judy with Mickey Rooney for the first time. The chemistry between the two is obvious. They play off each other's energy and (as they would in many future films) turn a paper-thin plot into an enjoyable vehicle.

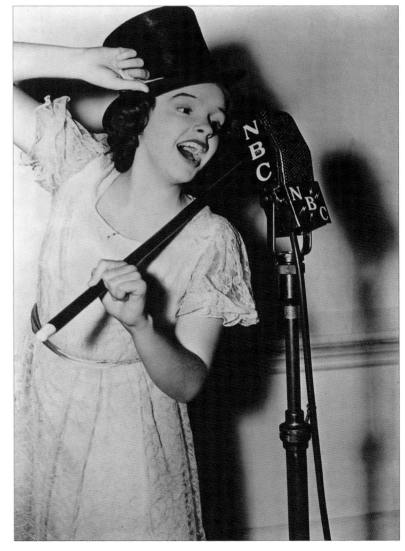

Above: *Everybody Sing* (1938) was shot at the same time as *Thoroughbreds Don't Cry*. Judy costarred with Broadway legend Fanny Brice (left). The reviews for the film were tepid, but once again, Judy walked away with accolades.

Right: Judy was warmly praised during a seven-week promotional tour for *Everybody Sing*, and wowed *Variety* when she appeared at Lowe's State Theater in New York. The *Variety* reporter prophetically wrote, "Youngster is a resounding wallop. . . . Apparent from the outset that girl is no mere flash, but has both the personality and the skill to develop into a box-office wow in any line of show business. Applause was solid and she encored twice, finally begging off with an ingratiating and shrewd thank you speech." Judy Garland had remembered and heeded the experiences of Baby Gumm.

Above: *Everybody Sing* was originally titled *The Ugly Duckling*. The name was changed to draw less attention to what MGM perceived were Judy's defects. Her body was short and chunky with practically no waist. Makeup and wardrobe could only do so much. The rest was handled with dieting and Benzedrine (prescribed by an MGM physician). It seems amazing, but at that time no one saw a problem with putting a teenager on drugs to make her slimmer for the camera.

Opposite, bottom: It is likely that Judy never took the bite antici-pated in this 1937 publicity photo. Her official diet included items such as clear broth and cottage cheese. MGM informants noti-fied executives if she ate fattening food, so she mischievously took to hiding cookies and candy bars when people weren't looking. It is particularly tragic when one considers how years later she would hide drugs in the same fashion.

Below: Judy's next film, *Love Finds Andy Hardy* (1938), again teamed her with Mickey Rooney. This time she was Betsy Booth, a char-acter whose love for Andy Hardy (played by Rooney) is never recognized or returned. Betsy is Andy's pal and confidant, nothing more. He spends his time pursuing Cynthia (Lana Turner, right) and Polly (Ann Rutherford, center). It's a well-played litany of snubs for touching comic effect.

eft: Judy's performance in *Love Finds Andy Hardy* was poignant and not totally acted. One day Maxine Marx (Chico's daughter) found Judy crying in the ladies' room. "I'm so ugly. Look at Annie and Lana." Maxine tried to console her. "But they have none of your talent. You're the one who has it all." Judy tearfully replied, "Who cares?"

bove: In Judy's sixth feature, *Listen, Darling* (1938), she played a girl whose mother is about to marry the wrong man. Once again life and art were eerily parallel. At that time Ethel was dating Will Gilmore, an old friend from Lancaster. To Judy's horror, they eloped on November 17, 1939. It was Ethel's birthday and the anniversary of Frank's death. This and other incidents drove a wedge between Judy and her mother that eventually became permanent estrangement.

Left: Volumes have been written about *The Wizard of Oz* (1939). It was certainly an important picture for MGM, but no one anticipated it would become a classic. Many of the film's most endearing elements were either late additions or almost cut, and that included Judy (shown here with Ray Bolger, Jack Haley, and Bert Lahr). MGM seriously considered Shirley Temple for the role of Dorothy, but Twentieth Century Fox would not loan Temple out.

Below: This is the first incarnation of the little girl from Kansas. She had blonde hair, a doll-like face, and was very solemn. Oz's first director, Richard Thorpe, was taken off the job after two weeks of shooting. His replacement, George Cukor, created the Dorothy we know today. He put her hair in braids, changed her dress, and told her not to act in a "fancy-schmancy way."

George Cukor left *The Wizard of Oz* to direct *Gone With the Wind* (1939). His replacement, Victor Fleming, did the bulk of the film (and then replaced Cukor on *Gone With the Wind*). Under Fleming's direction the beloved and renowned interplay between the Oz characters developed. Judy later poked fun at the way her costars supposedly competed with her for screen space, but in truth it was a perfect balance. She brilliantly played a regular little girl lost in a very irregular place.

Left: *Babes in Arms* (1939) again paired Judy with Mickey Rooney. The explosion of talent was delightful. They could sing, dance, act, do impressions, and generally provide nonstop entertainment. Script? Plot? It was all just a vehicle for screen high jinks. This film is the first of many blockbusters produced by Arthur Freed. It was the first time Judy worked with director Busby Berkeley. It was also the first rendition of the immortal story device "Hey! Let's put on a show!"

Right: You won't see this scene in rental copies of *Babes in Arms*. It was cut in a 1948 rerelease and never restored. Mickey did an impression of FDR and Judy played his wife, Eleanor. Here and in subsequent films the two young actors were constantly cutting up, making jokes, and generally infusing the staid production process with high-energy humor. Some of their impromptu antics (like stepping on each other's feet during a dance sequence) survived the editor's scissors and can still be seen.

Above: Louis B. Mayer looks benevolently upon his two young stars in this 1939 photo. He had great reason to smile: Judy's films grossed millions at the box office and he was paying her only $350 per week.

Left: About to take the plunge (from left to right) are Marjorie Gestring, Jackie Cooper, Judy, Mickey Rooney, June Preisser, and Virginia Weidler. This was Judy's "official" seventeenth birthday party, hosted by Louis B. Mayer. The unofficial party was at her home the day before. There she and her mother hosted comic actor Phil Silvers and his friend, bandleader Artie Shaw. Judy developed a serious romantic affection for Shaw early in 1939.

Right: Artie Shaw (shown here with Lana Turner) was twenty-eight years old. He was twice divorced and had a libidinous reputation, but his friendship with Judy was only flirtatious. They discussed books, music, and show business. They drove around Hollywood with friends. It never occurred to him that she would be crushed when he unexpectedly eloped with Lana Turner in February 1940.

Left: *Andy Hardy Meets Debutante* (1940) was produced in the middle of Judy's adolescent turmoil over Artie Shaw. Once again she played Betsy Booth, the girl whom Andy ignores. This time his attentions were focused on Diane Lewis (pictured here). The parallels were painful. In hindsight it is tempting to minimize Judy's discomfort. After all, she was a star. She had just won a special Oscar for her role in *The Wizard of Oz*, and the world was at her feet. But she was also seventeen years old and sensitive.

Judy, like many girls her age, wanted to be sexy like Lana Turner. In spite of her success, Judy didn't see herself as attractive. When MGM drama coach Lillian Burns told her she was talented and could do anything, Judy replied, "Except one thing. Except that when I sit down at a table opposite a man, all he can see is my head. I haven't any neck."

In *Strike Up the Band* (1940), Judy was again cast as an underappreciated girl next door. In this scene Mickey is apologizing for his attentions to June Preisser. Judy plays the moment with a perfect balance of pathos and latent comedy.

udy's endearing performance was reflected at the box office.
Strike Up the Band cost less than $1 million to make and grossed
nearly $3.5 million in its first release.

Left: Judy's eighteenth birthday was celebrated at Louis B. Mayer's home. Once again Mayer had reason to beam. The combined gross of Judy's films had reached well into the tens of millions, yet he was paying her only $500 per week. In September 1940 her contract was extended and renegotiated. Her weekly salary jumped to $2,000.

Right: *Little Nellie Kelly* (1940) is another example of a tepid story lifted to dramatic and comic heights by Judy's performance. Here (with George Murphy), she plays the only death scene of her career. Murphy later said that the production crew was so affected by her performance they had to clear the set "so that their sobs would not disturb or disrupt the sound track." *Little Nellie Kelly* was Judy's first adult role and featured her first screen kiss.

Left: Judy (pictured here with Jackie Cooper) got the full glamour treatment in *Ziegfeld Girl* (1941). Her costumes and makeup rivaled those of her sexy female costars, but Judy was disappointed with the result. The production crew would whistle when Lana Turner or Hedy Lamar walked past, but for Judy it was just a cheerful "Hi!"

Right: Teenage angst aside, Judy loved to laugh, especially when it was forbidden. Her costar Mary Astor said Judy "got the giggles regularly" during production of *Listen, Darling*. Here, she shares a giggle with music director George Stoll on the set of *Life Begins for Andy Hardy* (1941).

Babes on Broadway (1941) was a sequel of sorts to *Babes in Arms*.
The characters and situations are different, but the result is the
same. At some point Mickey shouts, "Hey! Let's put on a show!"
The kids do (more than once) and it becomes a wonderful excuse
for us to see Judy and Mickey singing and dancing with abandon.

eft: Busby Berkeley (shown here demonstrating a dance step) was a brilliant director and choreographer, but working with him was not easy. He was insensitive to actors, treating them more like set props than people. This particularly irked Judy, who appreciated feedback. Berkeley's feedback often took the form of a shout: "Eyes! Eyes! Open them wide. I want to see your eyes." He had nothing to say about her performance, only the size of her eyes.

Right: David Rose was arranging music at NBC the day after Judy's heartbreak over Artie Shaw. She was (through her tears) rehearsing for a broadcast. Rose brought some chocolate cake to console her. It worked. They were married on July 28, 1941 (during the filming of *Babes on Broadway*). Within a few months the strain of divergent schedules was pulling them apart. The couple was divorced in 1944.

Below: *For Me and My Gal* was Gene Kelly's screen debut. Judy was one of the people who recommended Kelly for the role. During production, Busby Berkeley clashed with the new film actor, but Judy used her considerable influence to support Kelly and protect his budding MGM reputation. Her efforts helped launch one of cinema's greatest talents. Here, the two stars dance enchantingly to the film's title tune.

Above: *For Me and My Gal* (1942) is perhaps Judy's most under-rated effort. Critics often call the film sentimental and naive. They're right. The film was produced during the darkest days after the bombing of Pearl Harbor. Judy and Gene Kelly are turn-of-the-century vaudevillians who fall in love while the world falls into war. The performances are truly affecting, and it's all wrapped up in some of Busby Berkeley's finest and most visually intimate director-ial work.

Left: In 1942, as the Axis powers threatened to overrun the earth, Hollywood helped rally the troops. Judy was the first Hollywood star to entertain servicemen and -women after Pearl Harbor. Her efforts continued throughout the war in live performances and on the radio. By war's end she had encouraged and comforted millions of Americans.

Right: Judy could be tender, wholesomely sexy, vulnerable, and funny all at the same time (as she is shown here in *Presenting Lily Mars*). There was a beguiling honesty about her. When Arthur Freed introduced her to his new assistant, Stella Adler, Judy was eating an ice cream cone. The film star extended the cone in her right fist like a small child and virtuously said, "Do you want a lick?"

Below: MGM made *Girl Crazy*, the last Rooney and Garland feature, in 1943. The script was (for once) not insipid. Part of the movie was shot on location in the desert, where Judy and Mickey did a delightful number, "Could You Use Me." It is perhaps the best interplay ever between the two.

Opposite, top: Of course at one point Mickey shouts, "Hey! Let's put on a show!" The *Girl Crazy* (1943) finale was a typical Busby Berkeley extravaganza, and "Buzz" was typically insensitive to his actors (and also to music arranger Roger Edens). This time the result was different. Judy was no longer the wide-eyed ungrudging trouper of years past. She and Edens complained, and Berkeley was summarily dismissed by producer Arthur Freed.

Above: Sincere and self-deprecating humor made Judy enchanting. She was the girl who pressed her nose sadly (and comically) against the glass in *Everybody Sing*. She accidentally beat up the boy next door in *Meet Me in St. Louis* and used a garter to remember her left leg from her right in *Easter Parade* (1948). Judy was sweet, open, and always hopeful. Here, she puckers for Van Heflin in *Presenting Lily Mars* (1943).

Below: *Girl Crazy* marked a turning point for Judy. According to Joe Mankiewicz, "She was beginning to show these signs, not showing up on time and taking too much Benzedrine, that sort of thing." It was part dependency and part rebellion. Judy had worked for MGM for nearly seven years. The studio told her what to eat, how to dress, whom to date, and how to live her life. Now she was twenty-one years old. For better or worse, things would change.

Chapter Three

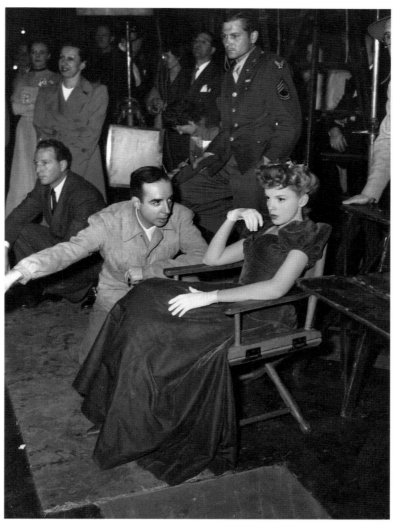

MGM Box Office Blockbuster

Opposite: *Meet Me in St. Louis* (1944) is generally regarded as one of Judy's best films, though she was initially unenthusiastic about the project. She was concerned because the script was a series of loosely connected episodes rather than a unified story. Judy also balked at playing the seventeen-year-old second sister, Esther, who falls in love with "the boy next door."

Above: Judy's misgivings were not lessened when George Cukor, the first director of *Meet Me in St. Louis*, was drafted into the armed forces and a relatively inexperienced Vincente Minnelli was chosen to replace him. After some initial friction (he had her stopped at the MGM gate when she tried to leave early), the two established a truce. In this photo, Minnelli offers direction to his petulant star.

Left: One of the most enchanting and complex scenes in *Meet Me in St. Louis* involves a long tracking shot through an Edwardian home. The camera follows Judy and her screen beau Tom Drake as they turn off gas lamps. The lights go down and the romantic tension rises. Minnelli was a highly cultured man who knew about such things as gas in antique chandeliers. Judy was twenty-one years old and (in spite of her many years at MGM) very impressed. Her animosity for Minnelli gave way to curiosity and eventually affection.

Right: Judy's cakewalk with Margaret O'Brien (shown here), "The Trolley Song," and the other loosely connected episodes of *Meet Me in St. Louis* came together to make the film a resounding success both critically and at the box office. It grossed $7.5 million in its first release (an MGM record). When Judy saw the film she recalled her initial concerns and commented to Arthur Freed, "Remind me not to tell you what kind of pictures to make."

Judy's next film was a remarkable departure from her earlier projects. *The Clock* (1945) was not a musical, but a romance. Judy plays an office worker and Robert Walker is a soldier who will soon be shipping out. Vincente Minnelli sensitively directed. The film received good reviews and grossed a reasonable $2.7 million, but that seemed paltry to MGM compared to the $7.5 million gross of *Meet Me in St. Louis*. Judy never made another straight dramatic film at the studio.

In *The Harvey Girls* (1946), Judy returned to the familiar (and profitable) musical-comedy format and played a frontier waitress. Her competition is bad girl Angela Lansbury (right). The result is a series of inspired comic moments, including this one where Judy single-handedly holds up a saloon to retrieve a stolen cache of beef. The raid is so inept that the saloon patrons offer directions about how to proceed, and they even help her complete the task.

Right: The onscreen hilarity of *The Harvey Girls* was in contrast to the actual mood on the set. According to costume designer Helen Rose, Judy was "slim and talented, but strung tight like a violin string." Patterns of behavior that began during *Meet Me in St. Louis* became more pronounced. She often called in sick or arrived late. According to Judy, "I was a nervous wreck, jumpy and irritable from sleeping too little. I couldn't take the tension at the studio."

Left: Judy's twenty-third birthday party was held on the set of *The Harvey Girls*. By this time her relationship with Vincente Minnelli had deepened into love. The two were married five days later on June 15, 1945. The man on the right in this shot, Arthur Freed, produced most of Judy's hits at MGM. The photo's awkward grouping is symbolic of Judy's increasingly troubled relationship with the studio. Freed seems affably unaware that his star is having a private moment. He just wants his cake.

Left: Judy was four months pregnant when she performed this small but critically praised role in *Till the Clouds Roll By* (1945). According to Gallup, she was Hollywood's third most popular female star. Only Ingrid Bergman and Bette Davis topped her. Judy's films grossed millions (she was earning $2,500 a week). In October 1945 she began a one-year hiatus. Daughter Liza May Minnelli was born on March 12, 1946.

Right: *The Pirate* (1948) marked Judy's return to pictures. Unfortunately, her problems returned, too. Judy was thin, unhappy, and abusing prescription drugs. The result was disastrous. She began work on *The Pirate* in December 1946 and didn't finish until one year later. The interim included two stays in sanitariums. Here she is pursued by Gene Kelly.

Director Vincente Minnelli did painful double duty, watching his wife disintegrate at work and at home. As *The Pirate* went perilously over-budget his relationship with Judy was tremendously strained. Still, there were moments of mirth and inspired creativity. While filming the song "Be a Clown" for *The Pirate*, Minnelli made the mighty discovery that Judy was beguiling in baggy clothes. For years MGM used expensive costumes to make her look more appealing, but it seems a stick of greasepaint and some oversize pants were more effective. The result energized Judy. Set designer Jack Martin Smith recalled, "She and Minnelli screamed and screamed with laughter."

Above: Judy's therapy revealed deep-seated resentment of authority figures, and one of those figures was Vincente Minnelli. Her doctor suggested she avoid working with her husband, so Arthur Freed (left) sacked Minnelli from Judy's next picture, *Easter Parade*. Minnelli would eventually direct many blockbusters for Freed, including *An American in Paris* (1951). Judy would do two more films for the famous producer, but the three were finished as a team.

Left: At the end of 1947 Judy began work on *Easter Parade*, and it seemed she was recovering. Here, she sings with composer Irving Berlin. Her hands are affectionately on Louis B. Mayer's shoulders while Arthur Freed happily looks on. The mood seems oddly more suited to a decade earlier.

Right: Gene Kelly was originally cast to play opposite Judy in *Easter Parade*, but he broke his ankle. Fred Astaire came out of retirement to replace him. Astaire's polished maturity and Judy's youthful exuberance created intoxicating screen chemistry. Their dancing was perfect. According to Astaire, "I go through all these intricate dance steps. She asks me to go through them again. That's all the instruction she needs."

Left: Building on the success of "Be a Clown," Judy again donned baggy clothes for the song and dance "A Couple of Swells." Again the result was inexplicably wonderful. It was Judy personified: youthful in spirit, impish, vulnerable, lovable, yet incorrigible. Director Charles Walters said, "All I had to do was stand back and let it happen." Judy loved the effect. Dressing like a "swell" would remain in her repertoire the rest of her life.

Right: Judy and Mickey Rooney made one last MGM appearance together in 1948. Louis B. Mayer offered Judy $50,000 to do one song with Rooney in *Words & Music* (1948). She was sick at the time, taking glucose intravenously. Judy removed the needle, went to the studio, and performed the song. It is ironic that MGM paid her more for one song than for her entire performance in *The Wizard of Oz*.

Left: Drug abuse and related poor health made Judy unpredictable. She was suspended from *The Barkleys of Broadway* after missing an entire week of shooting. At the time of her appearance in *Words & Music* she had withered to 85 pounds, but by late 1948 her health improved considerably. As a result MGM cast Judy opposite Van Johnson in *In The Good Old Summertime* (1949) a musical remake of the 1940 film *The Shop Around The Corner*.

ight: *In the Good Old Summertime* was a professionally tranquil period for Judy, and it marked a return to familiar and legendary work habits. She would read a script once, then perfectly remember the lines. She learned dance routines in one or two runthroughs. The film was completed ahead of schedule, and was hailed by *Newsweek* as "one of her best straight comedy performances." The film is also notable because the last scene features Liza Minnelli (shown here with "Mama") in her screen debut.

elow: Early in 1949, MGM celebrated its twenty-fifth anniversary with a star-studded party. Judy sat near Clark Gable, the man who had helped launch her career. He leaned over and said, "Goddamn brat. You've ruined every one of my birthdays. They bring you out of the wallpaper to sing that song, and it's a pain in the ass." She later reflected, "I've only begun to like him today, now that he's leveled with me."

Left: The rest of 1949 was extremely difficult for Judy. She had predictable problems with director Busby Berkeley on *Annie Get Your Gun* (1950). After a month of conflict he was replaced, but Judy was so upset and ill that she couldn't continue work. MGM suspended her one week later. Shortly thereafter she went to a Boston hospital for drug rehabilitation. Then, in late summer, she began work on *Summer Stock* (1950), shown here. It would be her last picture for MGM.

Right: *Summer Stock* (1950) is about some young theater folk who save a show by staging it in a barn. Sound familiar? Producer Joe Pasternak originally wanted Mickey Rooney for the role, but studio executives preferred Gene Kelly. Kelly did not relish doing a warmed-over version of *Babes on Broadway*, but he loved Judy. He also remembered her invaluable help on his first film.

Left: Director Charles Walters recalled, "Gene took her left arm and I took her right arm, and between us we literally tried to keep her on her feet." It took six difficult months to complete *Summer Stock*. The famous "Get Happy" sequence (shown here) was shot last, after Judy returned from a holiday. She was so slim (compared to earlier footage) that rumors persisted for years that the sequence was an outtake from a previous film.

Right: Judy shares a private moment with Liza on the set of *Summer Stock*. After the film's completion, Judy was cast in *Royal Wedding* (1951), but she was unable to perform. Once again the studio suspended her. That prompted an abortive suicide attempt, and then a strange calm. It seems Judy was happier when she wasn't working for MGM. One year later (at her request) she was released from her contract. In the end it was Judy who fired MGM.

Chapter Four

A Stage Star Is Born

Opposite: On August 12, 1951, Judy returned from London on the ocean liner *HMS Queen Elizabeth*. Her difficulties with MGM were in the past, and so was her marriage to Vincente Minnelli. A new relationship and a new stage career were bringing important changes. Judy seemed happy. Bing Crosby recalled, "She laughed infectiously." In her own words, "I never felt better in my life."

Above: The previous few months had seen a major success at the London Palladium. Judy wowed them in concert. She was plumper than in her films, but her unaffected stage presence was endearing. She chatted with the audience, sipped water, and took off her shoes. *Sight and Sound* called it "an extraordinary mixture of humor, vitality and sincerity of feeling." Judy had taken the first steps in redefining the concept of the modern pop concert.

October 16, 1951, at the Palace Theater, New York City. The second act began with a group of male dancers performing a routine. They gathered and parted. Judy appeared in their midst. A wave of recognition went through the audience. The house exploded in applause, stopping the show. It went on minute after minute until she finally shouted, "Hello" through the noise and continued. The concert was a tour de force and included favorites like "You Made Me Love You" and "Get Happy."

Above: Judy danced to "A Couple of Swells," then came to the footlights in her tramp costume. She sat in a small spotlight and performed the one song everyone had waited to hear. On the last strains of "Over the Rainbow," the audience exploded in a cacophony of applause. It lasted ten minutes as they strained to acknowledge inexplicable emotions. The Garland legend had been born.

Left: The person responsible for Judy's nineteen-week Palace engagement and much of her success in the post-MGM years was her third husband, Sid Luft. He was unlike any man Judy had previously known. Luft was a former test pilot with a reputation for action (and occasional brawling). He was not the type to mince words. Humphrey Bogart didn't think he had "class," but Judy loved him. They were married on June 8, 1952.

Left: In 1952 Judy (here with Lana Turner) turned thirty years old. The highs and the lows were coming more frequently. Daughter Lorna was born in November. Judy, driven by postpartum depression and drug abuse, slashed her own throat in December. She quickly recovered only to learn in January that her mother, Ethel Gumm, had died. Meanwhile, the greatest project of Judy's adult career was moving toward reality. Sid Luft had made an agreement with Warner Bros. to produce *A Star Is Born* (1954).

Below: She is a star on her way up. He is her husband, an alcoholic, and a star on his way down. *A Star Is Born* is regarded by many as Judy's finest screen work. George Cukor directed, and Harold Arlen (who wrote "Over the Rainbow") composed the music. Cary Grant was the original choice to play Norman Maine, but he declined the role. James Mason (shown here) was cast instead.

Left: Production was predictably troubled. Judy's old fears returned. She was brilliant in front of the camera, but getting her there was a challenge. Cukor (shown here) once went to coax his wayward star from her dressing room. He asked, "Is anything wrong?" Judy replied, "This is the story of my life. I'm about to shoot myself, and I'm asked if anything is wrong."

Right: In spite of production problems (some of which were not Judy's doing) an amazing picture was produced. *A Star Is Born* unflinchingly exposes the allure, intrigue, and absurdity of the movie business. Many of the scenes eerily reflect Judy's real experiences. Here, Norman (James Mason) fails to recognize Esther (Judy). She has been "improved" by the studio makeup department. When Norman realizes his mistake he bursts into laughter and removes the makeup.

The film is a motherlode of memorable scenes: Esther's uncomfortably genuine sobs recounting Norman's problems; the intimate and haunting "The Man That Got Away"; the proposal scene (which was cut in a subsequent release); the famous "Born in a Trunk" medley; and this scene in which Esther tries to cheer up Norman after he has been sacked by the studio.

Below: *A Star Is Born* opened to critical acclaim. Jack Warner (left) was tremendously pleased until he realized that the box office receipts were not as glowing as the reviews. The film's triple-budget overrun and three-hour length made profits difficult. In response Warner cut the film by twenty-seven minutes. The cuts were poorly handled and enraged the critics.

Right: Warner Bros.' cuts and the studio's subsequent lack of publicity for *A Star Is Born* doomed the film in the 1954 Oscars. It was nominated in six categories (including Judy as best actress), but it captured none of the awards. Grace Kelly took the best actress Oscar for *The Country Girl*. In this photo, Judy, Marlon Brando, and Edmond O'Brien have just received Golden Globe Awards.

By 1955 Judy had three children: Liza, Lorna, and Joey (born the day before the Oscars). The costs of keeping a celebrity family were mounting. Judy's troubled reputation discouraged film offers. She had a record contract, but that wasn't enough. She and Sid Luft (shown here with Liza in 1954) needed to generate income. So they said goodbye to films and hello to television.

L eft: On September 24, 1955, Judy did her first television special, the "Ford Star Jubilee" on CBS. Sid Luft produced and David Wayne (shown here) was the host and performed two of the numbers, "For Me and My Gal" and "A Couple of Swells," with Judy. The rest of the show was similar to her stage act. So was the audience response: twenty-five million Americans tuned in.

B elow: Judy and Humphrey Bogart share a chuckle in Las Vegas. Both were members of the infamous Rat Pack, a term coined by Lauren Bacall. Other members included Frank Sinatra, Dean Martin, Peter Lawford, and Judy's husband, Sid Luft (who was friends with Bogey in spite of the remarks about "class"). Late-night carousing and voluminous alcohol consumption characterized most Rat Pack activities.

Above: Seven years after their last MGM appearance together, Judy and Mickey posed for this picture in Las Vegas. The last decade had seen Judy's drug problems worsen. She was regularly taking Seconal, Dexedrine, Benzedrine, and a pharmacy cabinet of other pills and concoctions. Alcohol was also a problem. Sid Luft could only stand by and watch as Judy slid deeper into dependency.

Right: Judy returned to the Palace in the fall of 1956. She was heavier than ever, but the audience didn't seem to mind. *The New York Times* said, "The songs begin so informally and gather such vocal warmth and volume as she puts her heart into them that you would swear she was improvising." Once again she donned baggy clothes, this time to perform "Be a Clown," and then she sang the inevitable and anticipated "Over the Rainbow."

bove: Of the numerous people who loved and supported Judy throughout her life, few did so as consistently and completely as Sid Luft. By all accounts Luft was not a saint, but then (as the Hoagy Carmichael song she took her name from states) neither was Judy. The arguments were neverending. Luft was long-suffering, but he stuck with Judy and kept her head above water (and out of the toilet when she was ill) on many occasions. Here, Sid and Judy celebrate the new year: 1957.

eft: Judy performed in Las Vegas for the first time in 1956. She attracted capacity crowds then, and again a year later. Pearl Bailey recalled, "Judy took the place by the corners and shook it." Here, little Lorna sings "Jingle Bells" at the Flamingo Hotel, much as her mother had done thirty-two years earlier.

Below: The next two years were a study in contrasts for Judy. In the fall of 1957 she insisted on performing in London despite low ticket prices, which she knew would guarantee a financial loss. Her voice was strong and her reviews stupendous, but her frame had ballooned considerably. A subsequent Christmas booking in Las Vegas did not go well, nor did an engagement in Brooklyn the following spring. Both appearances were marred by disagreements with management.

Above: Judy dazzled the house at the Cocoanut Grove in July 1958. They loved her at New York's Metropolitan Opera House in May 1959. In the interim she performed in Chicago, Las Vegas, Miami, and Baltimore. The critics gushed, but the years of drug and alcohol abuse had taken their toll. Her liver was giving out. When she entered a hospital late in 1959, doctors believed she was close to death.

Chapter Five

Back from the Brink

Opposite: March 12, 1960: Liza's fourteenth birthday. Judy was out of the hospital and back from the brink. Her weight was down. Her only medication was Ritalin. The news spread that Judy was recovering. She performed concerts in the U.K. and Europe that summer and fall. Upon her return to the Palladium, Britain's *Daily Herald* said the response "shook stagehands hardened by years of hysterical audience reaction."

Above: Judy was such an admirer of John F. Kennedy that she toured U.S. bases in the fall of 1960 promoting his campaign. Her support undoubtedly helped in his subsequent narrow victory. The new president remembered her contribution and occasionally he would call Judy on the phone and request she sing "Over the Rainbow."

Judy returned to the U.S. with Liza, Lorna, and Joey on December 31, 1960. She was ready to resume work on stage, on television, and even in films. Judy had new agents, Freddie Fields and David Begelman (both formerly of MCA), who would play instrumental roles in her revitalized career. They would also be unintentional catalysts for her eventual divorce from Sid Luft.

ight: *Judgment at Nuremberg* (1961) marked Judy's return to the silver screen. It was her first straight dramatic role since *The Clock*, her first film since 1954, and her first supporting role since her teen years. The courtroom drama featured an all-star cast, including Spencer Tracy and Burt Lancaster. Judy played a German woman who testifies about Nazi crimes. Stanley Kramer brilliantly directed her to an Oscar-nominated performance.

eft: When she arrived on the set of *Judgment at Nuremberg*, the crew broke into spontaneous applause. Stanley Kramer (shown here directing) described Judy as "a piano. You touch any key, and a pure note of emotion comes out." The shoot proceeded on schedule. When it finished, Judy resumed a national concert tour.

Above: Judy's 1961 tour is considered by many to be the high point of her concert career, particularly the April performance at Carnegie Hall. *Variety* reported that the frenzied audience members "pressed against the stage begging for more at the end of her two and a half hour show." Merv Griffin said of the Carnegie Hall experience, "Nothing in show business will ever top it. No Broadway opening, film premiere, nothing."

Left: Judy returned to CBS television in early 1962 for a special that was titled simply "The Judy Garland Show." Dean Martin and Frank Sinatra were guests. The format was uncomplicated: just singing and more singing. It worked. The show's success in the ratings against NBC's hit *Bonanza* laid the groundwork for the TV series Judy would do one year later.

Judy's life was becoming hectic. In the spring of 1962 she did *A Child Is Waiting* (1963), another dramatic film with Burt Lancaster. In this film she plays a music teacher at a school for retarded children. Lancaster is the school principal, and they disagree about how to handle the students. The subject of children with disabilities was close to Judy's heart. She supported many youth-related charities, and frequently hosted and performed at fund-raising events.

After finishing *A Child Is Waiting*, Judy began work on what would be her final film. *I Could Go On Singing* (1963). By this point Judy's tempestuous relationship with Sid Luft had turned acrimonious. The couple had separated numerous times. Fields and Begelman (now known as CMA) supplanted Luft professionally. They booked Judy's gigs and arranged her accommodations. Luft was often left wondering where his wife and children were. A bitter child custody battle erupted.

Stress and a starring role had caused Judy problems in the past, and they did so again. She performed well but behaved badly. The result was barely enough footage to complete *I Could Go On Singing*. It opened to generally good reviews but, curiously, did poorly at the box office. In the next few years other film roles would be considered (including *Valley of the Dolls* [1967]) but nothing ever materialized on the screen. Judy's film career was over.

Left: Robert Goulet and Phil Silvers were guests on Judy's television special on March 19, 1963. CBS billed it as a preview/pilot of her upcoming fall TV series. In contrast to the previous specials, this time CBS wanted banter and comedy along with singing. Judy was a gifted actress and hilariously funny, so it was no problem. The critics mostly raved. The ratings were good, but the network's sudden focus on joviality was a sign of bad things to come.

Right: Mickey Rooney helped inaugurate Judy's TV series, *The Judy Garland Show*, on June 24, 1963. Two decades after *Girl Crazy* the magic still worked and wacky happiness reigned. Mickey sang "Thank Heaven for Little Girls" surrounded by tall beauties. He and Judy teamed up for "Can You Use Me" and a medley of other songs. Judy closed the show with "Old Man River." Hedda Hopper gleefully said it "took you right back to the old Andy Hardy days."

Below: Liza performed professionally with Judy for the first time on *The Judy Garland Show*. At seventeen years of age Liza was taking her first steps into what would be a luminous career in entertainment. Judy loved her children and supported her elder daughter's aspirations, but didn't relinquish her motherly prerogatives. That included an attempt to keep Liza out of a stage show when the teen was recuperating from an illness. Judy sent a telegram to the producer and issued a press release stating Liza would not perform, but the strong-willed young woman did the show anyway.

Above: Tony Bennett was Judy's guest on the fifth taped episode. Here they sing a stirring rendition of "I Left My Heart in San Francisco." Judy was in fine voice and excellent spirits. The pairing with Bennett was sensational. CBS, however, was not pleased: note Judy's hand on Bennett's knee—the network believed Judy touched her guests too much.

Above: None of the episodes had yet been aired, but CBS felt it was all wrong. They believed Judy was too distant. The network executives wanted a "girl next door." She didn't talk enough. They didn't like her choice of guests. She wanted Count Basie, Lena Horne, and Barbra Streisand (shown here). CBS preferred George Maharis and Zina Bethune. The network fired the show's creative staff without warning, and set about making a "new" Judy Garland.

Right: No more touching the guests. Now Judy would sip tea and talk with them in a special segment, as she does here with Ray Bolger. The programs were rigidly formatted into "standard compartments" that CBS felt audiences needed. (Decades later, David Letterman would make a career of lampooning the style of transparent television posturing that was imposed onto Judy's show.) The network had no faith in her creative instincts. In their words, "She knows we know what is good for her."

Right: Judy (shown here performing the "couple of swells" routine with Liza) could have quit after the network meddling (her contract allowed her to cancel after thirteen episodes), but by 1963 she had become somewhat more pragmatic. Part of the reason for doing a television series was to put herself and her family on a firm financial footing. In spite of her fame, she was not a rich woman. She was tired of endless touring. Judy wanted a hit show and some piece of mind, so she gamely compromised with CBS.

Below: The result was a ratings disaster. *Bonanza* consistently trounced *The Judy Garland Show*. Critics and the American public knew something wasn't right. The *New York Times* called Judy "a prisoner of her own production." Still, there were moments of bliss: dancing with Donald O'Connor (shown here), clowning with Bob Newhart, and singing to Lorna and Joey. Judy's talents were never more evident, but CBS didn't notice. After twenty-six inspired but often difficult episodes, the show ended.

Above: As the television series died, a new relationship developed for Judy. He was Mark Herron, a thirty-one-year-old actor. Herron traveled with Judy on an ill-fated international concert tour in the summer of 1964. The low points included a notoriously bad show in Australia (many in the audience asked for a refund), a typhoon in Hong Kong, and a near-deadly drug overdose. After this nightmarish episode, Judy's health was never quite the same.

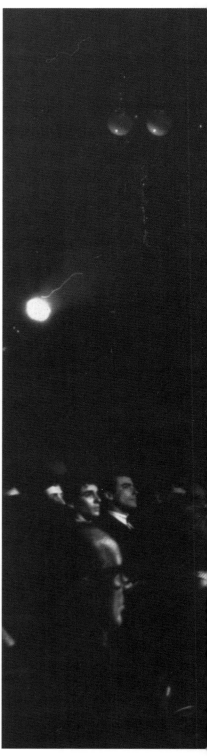

elow: London had always provided new beginnings for Judy, and it was to London she returned in 1964. There she unintentionally upstaged The Beatles at the "Night of a Hundred Stars" benefit. Judy was recuperating and not scheduled to perform, but the audience would not be denied. They stopped the show with applause until she sang. The resulting joyous pandemonium ended the program when The Beatles graciously (and wisely) declined to follow her. Other London appearances included *The Jack Paar Show* (shown here).

In the autumn of 1964 Liza joined Judy in London, and together they did a series of performances at the Palladium, two concerts, and one television special. At Liza's request a then-unknown Marvin Hamlisch arranged some of the music.

Judy sang "Hello Liza" to the tune of "Hello Dolly," and two generations shared the stage. Liza, the gifted child of extraordinary parents, would soon entertain millions and explore new levels of performance in film, theater, and music. She would win a Tony Award within a year, be nominated for an Academy Award before the end of the decade, and win the coveted Oscar for *Cabaret* in 1973. Here mother and daughter rehearse for the show.

Below: The years 1965 and 1966 marked a difficult turning point for Judy. Her life, always tumultuous, became even more troubled. The frequent separations from Sid Luft finally ended in divorce. She married Mark Herron, but the marriage lasted only a few months. Financial and health problems plagued her. Her lifelong abuse of drugs and alcohol was taking its toll. Judy worked less and fretted more. Yet there were still moments when Judy exhibited all of her legendary magic and mirth. Here she performs with Andy Williams on *The Andy Williams Show.*

Opposite: Of course, there was a comeback. There was always a comeback. It came in 1967 and was orchestrated by Sid Luft. Judy did a flurry of concerts across the country and made a celebrated return to the Palace (shown here). Lorna and Joey performed with her in New York and many of the other venues. Critics admitted her voice had dissipated, but her style was undiminished. The fans just loved her.

Stories from the last two years of Judy's life are bizarrely inconsistent, yet most are undeniably true. Some accounts have her thin as a wraith and unable to perform, or even speak clearly. Other descriptions paint her as full of gusto. Her last performance in the United States was on July 20, 1968, in Philadelphia. The *Philadelphia Inquirer* reported, "She held the audience in the palm of her hand from the first entrance."

L ike a bird in a hurricane, Judy struggled on. She did a few talk
shows and a few concerts. She married Mickey Deans, a night-
club manager in early 1969. She performed briefly in Sweden
and Denmark, then returned to London and prepared once again
for rejuvenation. This photo of her and Deans was taken during that
time. On June 22, 1969, Judy took some pills to help herself sleep,
then drifted away forever.

Conclusion

Yes, she was talented. She had a beautiful voice and great style. But her real genius was how she attracted and inspired so many other talented people who then lifted her up. Exceptional people loved Judy Garland exceptionally. Many of the twentieth century's greatest writers, directors, producers, composers, and performers, as well as countless other stage and screen professionals, contributed passionately to Judy's incomparable life. It was not just one woman on that lonely stage singing "Over the Rainbow." It was an amalgamation of the most inspired talent on earth.

The miracle is how the collaboration inexorably spread from the stage and screen to the audience. By the end of Judy's career the fans were singing to her. The people standing on their seats with tears streaming down their faces were as likely to be Hollywood stars as plumbers from Hoboken. Performer and audience were one. Another of Judy's contradictions? Of course.

pposite: It is a testament to the remarkable nature of Judy that so many people—fans, friends, and family—passionately love and protect her even to this day, in spite of the difficulties she inflicted on them. Why? Because interspersed among the problems were moments of bliss. Liza wrote of her mother, "The middle of the road was never for her. . . . If she was happy, she wasn't just happy; she was ecstatic. And when she was sad, she was sadder than anybody."

bove: So this is the Judy we remember, singing "Over the Rainbow." This is the Judy we love, rising from trouble and on her way to a happier and better place.

Filmography

Every Sunday (1936 short)
Pigskin Parade (1936)
Broadway Melody of 1938 (1937)
Thoroughbreds Don't Cry (1937)
Everybody Sing (1938)
Love Finds Andy Hardy (1938)
Listen, Darling (1938)
The Wizard of Oz (1939)
Babes in Arms (1939)
Andy Hardy Meets Debutante (1940)
Strike Up the Band (1940)
Little Nellie Kelly (1940)
Ziegfeld Girl (1941)
Life Begins for Andy Hardy (1941)
Babes on Broadway (1941)
For Me and My Gal (1942)
We Must Have Music (1942)
Presenting Lily Mars (1943)

Girl Crazy (1943)
Thousands Cheer (1943)
Meet Me in St. Louis (1944)
The Clock (1945)
The Harvey Girls (1946)
Till the Clouds Roll By (1946)
Ziegfeld Follies (1946)
The Pirate (1948)
Easter Parade (1948)
Words and Music (1948)
In the Good Old Summertime (1949)
Summer Stock (1950)
A Star Is Born (1954)
Pepe (1960, cameo)
Judgment at Nuremberg (1961)
A Child Is Waiting (1963)
I Could Go On Singing (1963)

Bibliography

Coleman, Emily R. *The Complete Judy Garland.* New York: Harper & Row, 1990.

Frank, Gerold. *Judy.* New York: Harper & Row, 1975.

Kaufman, Gerald. *Meet Me in St. Louis.* London: British Film Institute, 1994.

Leigh, Wendy. *Liza—Born a Star.* New York: Dutton, 1993.

Morella, Joe, and Edward Z. Epstein. *Judy — The Complete Films & Career of Judy Garland.* New York: Citadel Press, 1990.

Rooney, Mickey. *Life Is Too Short.* New York: Villard, 1991.

Shipman, David. *Judy Garland—The Secret Life of an American Legend.* New York: Hyperion, 1992.

Torme, Mel. *The Other Side of the Rainbow.* New York: William Morrow, 1970.

Watson, Thomas, and Bill Chapman. *Judy—Portrait of an American Legend.* New York: McGraw-Hill, 1986.

Photography Credits

Index